DAD
MY HERO

COMPENDIUM™
PUBLISHING

live inspired.

ACKNOWLEDGEMENTS

These quotations were gathered lovingly but unscientifically over several years and/or contributed by many friends or acquaintances. Some arrived—and survived in our files—on scraps of paper and may therefore be imperfectly worded or attributed. To the authors, contributors and original sources, our thanks, and where appropriate, our apologies. —The Editors

WITH SPECIAL THANKS TO

Jason Aldrich, Gloria Austin, Gerry Baird, Jay Baird, Neil Beaton, Josie Bissett, Chris Dalke, Jim Darragh, Jennifer & Matt Ellison, Rob Estes, Michael Flynn, Jennifer Hurwitz, Heidi Jones, Carol Anne Kennedy, Steve and Janet Potter & Family, Diane Roger, Drew Wilkie, Robert & Mary Anne Wilkie, Kristel Wills, Christy Wires, Heidi, Shale & Ever Yamada, Justi, Tote & Caden Yamada, Val Yamada, Kaz, Kristin, Kyle & Kendyl Yamada, Tai & Joy Yamada, Anne Zadra, August & Arline Zadra, Augie & Rosie Zadra.

CREDITS

Written by Dan Zadra & Kobi Yamada
Designed by Jenica Wilkie & Clarie Yam

MY HERO...

MY WORLD

When I was with my father, when I was just a child, the world was filled with wonder and every place was wild. And every day was magic, and Santa Claus was true, and all the things that mattered were things my father knew.

MARSHA JEFFREY HENDRICKSON

MY FOUNDATION

The history, the strength of my father,
is the foundation we now rest on.

UNKNOWN

MY CONFIDENCE

Whenever I try to recall that long-ago first day of school only one memory shines through: my father held my hand.

MARCELENE COX

MY ENCOURAGEMENT

I fell down the first time I tried to ride a bike. I nearly drowned the first time I tried to swim. Then came my father's soothing voice, "You can do it, nothing to it."

TONY SHAGAN

MY REFUGE

When I cried, he caught my tears.

JILEEN RUSSELL

MY MIRACLE WORKER

He could fix almost anything…
a broken wagon, or a broken heart.

DAN ZADRA

MY EXAMPLE

My father didn't tell me how to live;
he lived and let me watch him do it.

CLARENCE KELLAND

MY COACH

My dad always taught me
these words: care and share.

TIGER WOODS

MY CHAMPION

Whenever I did something…
learn to swim or act in a school play,
for instance—he was fabulous.
There would be this certain look in
his eyes. It made me feel great.

DIANE KEATON

MY BIGGEST FAN

There must have been hundreds of people cheering at some of those track meets, but my father's voice always found me. A simple, "That's it kid," and my feet grew wings.

MADISON RILEY

MY COMPASS

He showed me right from wrong.

JAMES EARLY

MY ADVISOR

The word "no" carries a lot more meaning when spoken by a father who also knows how to say yes.

JOYCE MAYNARD

MY ROCK

My father gave me the greatest gift anyone could give. He believed in me.

JIM VALVANO

MY DRIVE

Dad instilled in me the attitude of prevailing. If there's a challenge, go for it. If there's a wall to break down, break it down.

DON OSMOND

MY SPARK

Sometimes our light goes out but is blown into flame by another human being. Each of us owes deepest thanks to those who have rekindled this light.

ALBERT SCHWEITZER

MY ROLE MODEL

My father used to say there are
two kinds of people: those who stop
at an accident and those who drive by.
He was the kind who would help.
We're trying to follow his example.

MARLO THOMAS

MY STRENGTH

I think of my dad as the strongest man I've ever met because he's the kindest man I've ever met.

ANN ELIZABETH

MY FINANCIAL EXPERT

"If you want to feel rich,"
he would say, "just count
all the gifts you have
that money can't buy."

UNKNOWN

MY YARDSTICK

The measure of life is not
its duration but its donation.

PETER MARSHALL

MY LIGHT

No person was ever honored for what he received. Honor has been the reward for what he gave.

CALVIN COOLIDGE

MY INSPIRATION

Thanks for showing me that
even on the darkest, rainiest days
the sun is still there, just behind the
clouds, waiting to shine again.

LISA HARLOW

MY VALUES

His values embraced family,
reveled in the social mingling of
the kitchen, and above all, welcomed
the loving disorder of children.

JOHN COLE

MY JOY

That is the best: to laugh with someone because you both think the same things are funny.

GLORIA VANDERBILT

MY COMPANION

His hand on my shoulder,
his proud smile, his reassuring
wink. Dad had a thousand
ways to say "I love you"
without ever saying it at all.

JEROME RIGGS

MY BEST FRIEND

There is no friend like someone who has known you since the day you were born.

BILL HARTZELL

MY ROOTS

I don't mind looking into the mirror and seeing my father.

MICHAEL DOUGLAS

MY GREATEST INHERITANCE

His heritage to his children wasn't words or possessions, but an unspoken treasure, the treasure of his example as a man and a father.

WILL ROGERS, JR.

MY MEMORIES

All these years later, wherever I am,
I still hear your laughter, still feel
your love, still see your smile.

HELEN MARM

MY FUTURE

And though I know we are different,
I am grateful for what I have of my
father in me. It is my gift, my promise
to myself and my children.

KEN BARRETT

MY HERO

Dad, I love you not only for what you have made of yourself, but for what you are making of me.